Read-About® Geography

Map Keys

By Rebecca Aberg

Consultant
Jeanne Clidas, Ph.D.
National Reading Consultant
and
Professor of Reading, SUNY Brockport

SCHOLASTIC INC.

New York   Toronto   London   Auckland   Sydney
Mexico City   New Delhi   Hong Kong   Buenos Aires

Designer: Herman Adler Design
Photo Researcher: Caroline Anderson
The artwork on the cover shows a simple map and corresponding key.

ISBN 0-516-25542-8

12 11 10 9 8 7 6 5 4   5 6 7 8 9/0

Printed in the U.S.A.   61

First Scholastic printing, October 2004

What is a map key?

A map key is a box that is next to a map. It is also called a legend (LEG-uhnd).

MAP KEY

airport

fire
station

library

school

park

Pictures on maps are symbols (SIM-buhlz). A map key tells what the symbols mean.

Some symbols are pictures of things we know.

This map shows part of a town. Use the key to read the map.

What is the symbol for the school? Can you find the fire station?

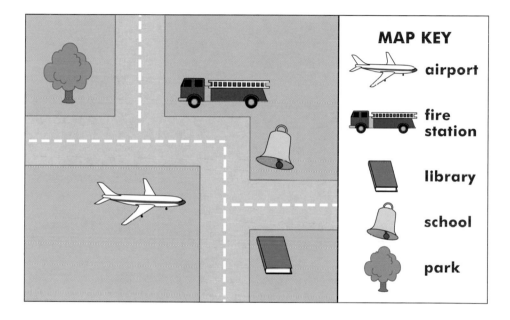

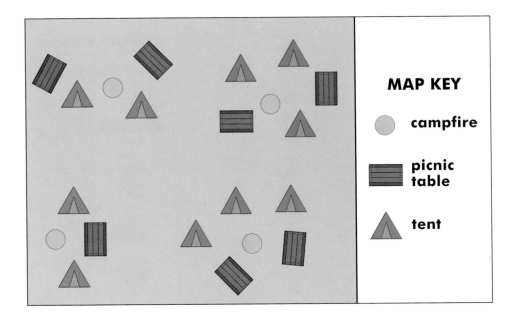

MAP KEY

- ⬤ campfire
- ▭ picnic table
- ▲ tent

Some symbols are shapes. The map key shows what each shape means.

This is a map of a campground. Triangles (TRIE-ang-guhls) stand for the tents. What do the circles stand for?

Other symbols are colors. The map key shows what each color means.

On this map, water is blue. Cities are yellow. What color is farmland?

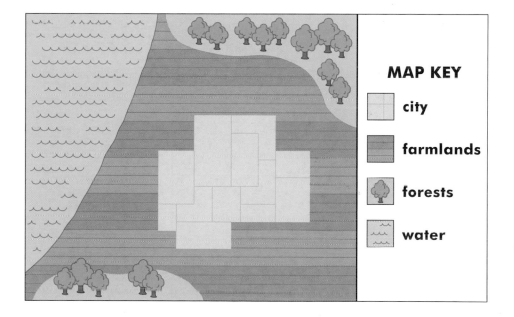

MAP KEY

city

farmlands

forests

water

13

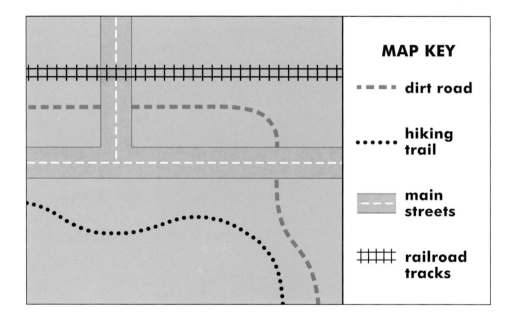

MAP KEY

▪ ▪ ▪ ▪ dirt road

•••••• hiking trail

main streets

railroad tracks

Some maps use different
kinds of lines as symbols.
These lines stand for
streets, hiking trails,
and railroad tracks.

Look at this map and map
key. What are the dotted
lines? Can you find the
railroad tracks?

Here is a map of a zoo. Use the map key to find Jungle Trail. What animals will you see along the trail?

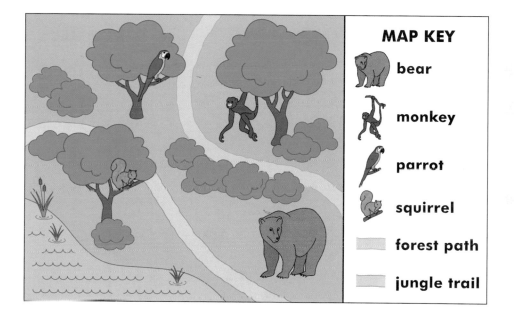

MAP KEY

bear

monkey

parrot

squirrel

forest path

jungle trail

17

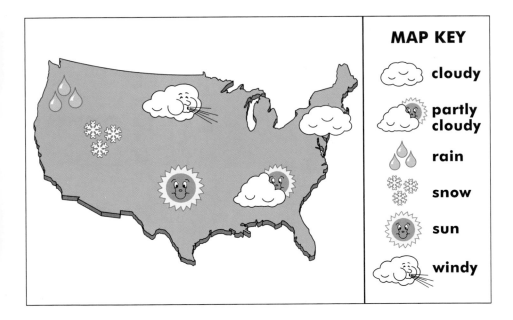

MAP KEY

cloudy

partly cloudy

rain

snow

sun

windy

Symbols on weather (WHETH-ur) maps show sun, clouds, rain, and snow.

Point to the places that are sunny. Where is it raining? What do the snowflakes mean?

Maps of rooms are called floor plans. These maps look like you are looking down from the ceiling. The top of a table may look like a rectangle (REK-tang-guhl).

What shape are the student desks on this floor plan?

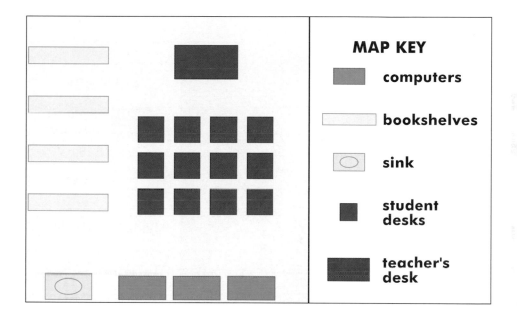

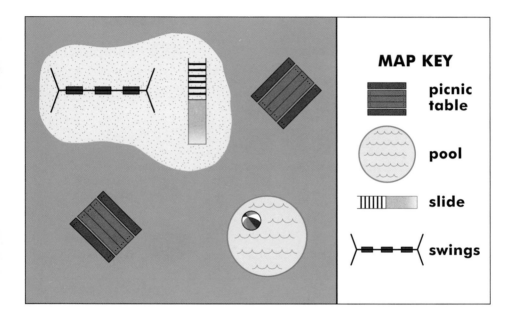

MAP KEY

picnic table

pool

slide

swings

Some floor plans show outdoor places.

Here is a map of a park. What symbols stand for the picnic tables? How many slides do you see?

Maps are fun to make.
You can draw a map of
your bedroom.

What is the shape of your
room? What shapes and
colors will you use for
the things in your room?

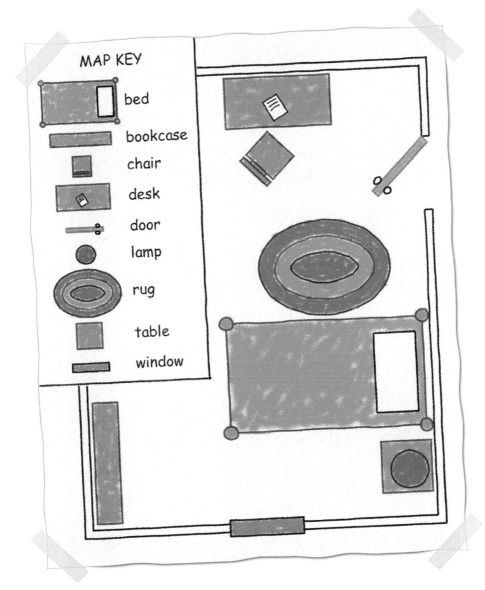

MAP KEY

bed

bookcase

chair

desk

door

lamp

rug

table

window

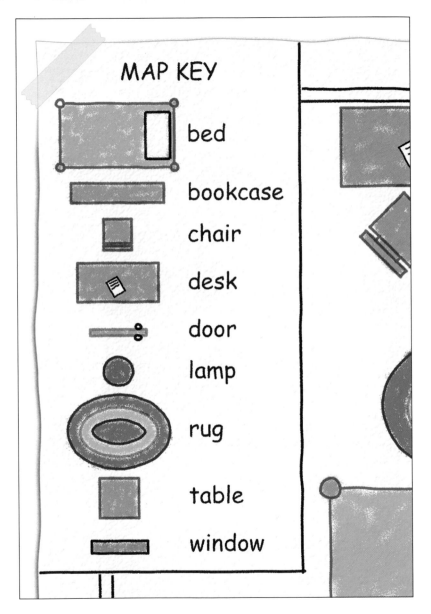

MAP KEY

bed

bookcase

chair

desk

door

lamp

rug

table

window

Don't forget to draw a map key for your bedroom map.

Use the same symbols you used on your map, only make them smaller. Write what each symbol means.

Now everyone can read
your map.

Words You Know

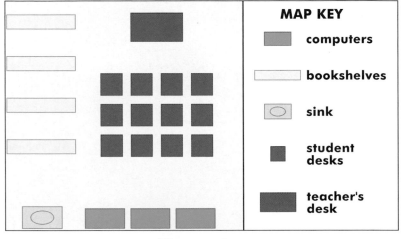

MAP KEY

computers

bookshelves

sink

student desks

teacher's desk

floor plan

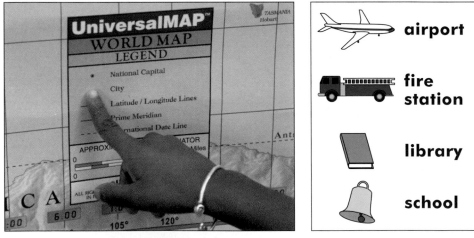

map key

airport

fire station

library

school

symbols

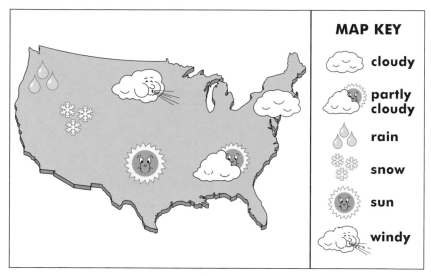

weather map

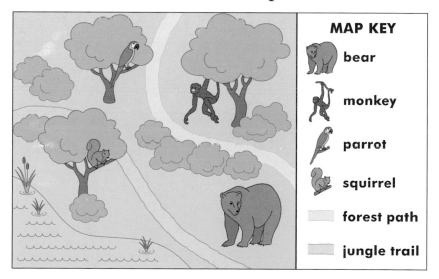

zoo map

31

Index

About the Author

Rebecca Aberg lives in Wisconsin and teaches elementary school. She has written more than 20 books. Rebecca enjoys learning as much as she enjoys teaching others.

Photo Credits

Photographs © 2003: Corbis Images/Richard Hutchings: 3; Leslie Barbour: 5, 30 bottom left; Photo Researchers, NY/Lawrence Migdale: 29.

Maps by XNR Productions